CW00869225

Birds

Contents

Nests

Birds do not live in their nests. They lay their eggs in them.

Blackbirds build their nests in trees or bushes. You may see a brown female blackbird collecting dry grass, twigs and moss. She uses these to build her nest in the branches of a low tree or bush. She sticks the materials together with lumps of wet mud.

After it has dried, the nest inside is as smooth as an empty coconut shell.

You may find three or four nests belonging to the same blackbird in one garden. The blackbird tests a nest for some days to see if it is quite safe and well hidden before she chooses which one to lay her eggs in.

Try to build a nest. Use pieces of grass, straw and leaves. Can you make it smooth and neat? Do birds build better nests than humans?

↗ Blue tits look for a safe place to lay their eggs. This might be a small crack in a hollow tree, a hole in a wall, or a wooden nesting-box hung in the garden. As long as the entrance is small and will not allow other birds or animals through, it will do.

Blue tits collect the softest leaves and mosses they can find to line the inside of the nest. This makes a warm and cosy bed for their young.

⭐ Weaver birds are possibly the best nest builders of all. The entrance to a weaver's nest is up a long tube woven with strips of leaves. It may be as much as 70 centimetres long.

Eggs

Some birds lay many eggs. The female mallard may lay as many as sixteen pale green or grey eggs.

When they hatch, the young are already well developed. They can see and their legs are strong so they can run after their mother.

The young mallards get into the water and feed themselves within a few hours. After about six weeks they are ready to fly.

Mallards eat the buds and stems of water plants. Their nests are usually on the ground. They are carefully hidden and made of leaves and grass.

The fossil of one of the biggest eggs in the world is in the Bristol Museum. It is the egg of an elephant bird which is now **extinct**. The egg is about one million years old.

Some birds lay smaller **clutches** of eggs. Robins lay three to six white speckled eggs and the young are born blind and naked. They grow quickly. The robin is kept busy fetching insects and worms to push into the mouths of the nestlings. They grow a coat of **down feathers**. But the young robins cannot fly until their flight feathers are formed. This takes 12 to 14 days.

Here are the eggs of some common birds. If you see eggs in a nest, leave them alone.

Robin

Starling

Blackbird

Thrush

Sparrow

How strong is eggshell?

Here is a simple way to test the strength of an eggshell. You can try it at school or at home.

You need to use a plastic bottle cut in half. Put half an eggshell in the bottom of the bottle. Use a hen's egg, or if you can find an eggshell that's already broken, use that. **Never take eggs out of birds' nests.**

Make sure that the neck of the bottle rests on the eggshell. Put some weights or sand into the top part.

How many weights or cups of sand do you think you will need to break the shell?

How many did you need?

Do all shells need the same number of weights or cups of sand before they break?

Sand or weights

Eggshell

Plastic bottle

An ostrich egg measures 15 centimetres long and weighs over one and a half kilograms. The shell is so thick that you could stand on it.

Rules for caring for wild birds

Write and design a poster to help protect and care for wild birds. Put five rules on your poster. Here are some questions which will help get you started. Can you think of some other rules?

1. If you find a nest with eggs in it, what should you do?

2. How can you help birds in winter?

Beaks and feet

The beaks and feet of birds help us tell what food birds eat and where they live.

The tufted duck has a broad wedge-shaped beak. This is just right for pulling out mouthfuls of tasty plants which grow in ponds and lakes. Tufted ducks like insects too and these are trapped in their beaks with the plants.

The large webbed feet of ducks are perfect for pushing them through the water and for walking on mud.

Tufted duck

Garden birds, like starlings and blackbirds, eat several kinds of food: berries, worms, insects, or food from the bird-table. Their beaks can do many different jobs.

Look at other birds' beaks. Do they help tell you what sort of food those birds eat?

Kestrels feed on mice and small birds. Their beaks are curved and sharp. They are specially shaped to pluck off feathers and fur. The kestrel can then tear off the flesh of the small animals.

Kestrels catch their prey with their feet. They have sharp **talons** which they use to snatch a bird from the air or a mouse from the ground.

The heron stands as still as a statue on its long legs. It waits for the ripple of an eel in shallow waters or the rustle of a mouse in the grass. The long sharp beak strikes like a pick-axe and the heron enjoys a tasty meal.

Some birds use their beaks as tools. Egyptian vultures hold stones in their beaks and use them to crack open the hard shells of ostrich eggs.

Joe and Gilly

Inspector White works for the RSPCA. The RSPCA helps sick and injured animals. Sometimes, mother animals abandon their cubs and the RSPCA takes them in and feeds them. Sometimes, people are cruel to their pets and the RSPCA rescues them. Sometimes, birds and animals are injured on the roads and the RSPCA looks after them.

2 At the RSPCA centre, there is a seagull with a broken wing.

1 Inspector White works in a seaside town. She looks after ordinary animals like cats and dogs. But she cares for unusual animals as well.

3 There is a baby seal, abandoned by its mother. Inspector White feeds it from a bottle, like a human baby. When the creatures are able to look after themselves, Inspector White will set them free.

4 One day a boy called Joe rang the RSPCA.

> I'm in the call-box by the beach. There's oil on the sand. A guillemot is covered in oil. It can't fly. It's exhausted.

5 Inspector White drove to the beach. She put the guillemot in a cage and loaded it into her van.

> Thanks for phoning. If you hadn't phoned this guillemot would have died.

6 Inspector White and Joe drove back to the RSPCA centre.

7 Inspector White put on gloves and a plastic mac. She poured warm water into a basin and added detergent. She filled another basin with clean, warm water. Then she opened the cage and laid the guillemot gently on the table.

9 Inspector White washed its feathers carefully with detergent. The detergent made the oil run off in streaks.

8 The guillemot was too exhausted to struggle. It lay on the table. It opened and closed its beak. It made no sound.

10 Then Inspector White rinsed the feathers with clean water.

11 When the oil was washed away, Inspector White clipped the guillemot's wings.

12 Slowly, Inspector White nursed the guillemot back to health. The bird's feathers regained their **sheen** and colour. Her wings grew strong new flying feathers.

It doesn't hurt. It will stop the guillemot flying away. She needs to rest and build up her strength It will take weeks or even months.

She'll be safe now.

13 At last it was time to let her go. Joe and Inspector White took her to the beach, and watched her fly away.

Identifying birds

Colour

The brown sparrow, the red breasted robin, the male blackbird with his bright yellow beak, and the black and white magpie are well known to us. The colours help us identify the different birds.

Robin

Sparrow

Magpie

Blackbird

Wings and tails

Look at a bird's outline when it is flying. The shape of its wings and tail will help you identify it.

Rooks, crows and ravens have broad wings. They are good for gliding and flying straight. The wing tips are spread like fingers.

Magpies are easy to spot high in the sky with their long unusual-shaped tails.

The swift's outline is very different. It has long, pointed, swept-back wings. These are perfect for fast flying and quick changes in direction. It eats insects and collects nest materials in mid-air. It has a long forked tail.

Bird shapes

Look at some birds flying in the sky. Draw their shapes.

Here are the outlines of some common birds. Do the outlines help you identify birds in the playground? How good are you at spotting birds in flight?

Sparrow

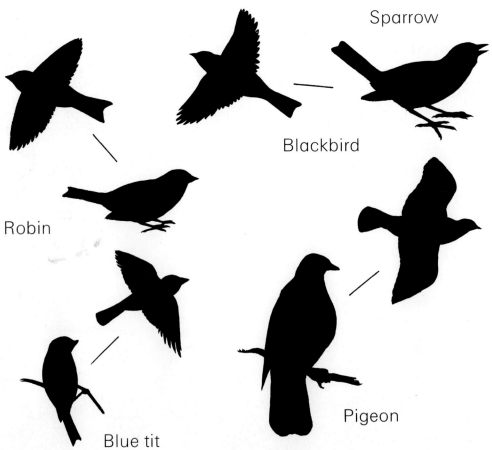

Blackbird

Robin

Pigeon

Blue tit

The Summer Show

There will be a great flying display,
Not to be missed,
In my garden,
To-morrow,
From dawn onwards.
Two swallows,
Promise to make a summer of it,
The magpies will provide a commentary,
From the upper branches of the birch tree,
Whilst the sparrows
Will make stand-by flights,
From gutter to gutter.
Don't miss it!

John Cunliffe

Flocks of birds

Some birds live alone, but other birds like to keep in large groups or **flocks**.

You won't often see two robins at the same time. Robins like to live alone. In late winter the female begins to look for a mate but she is not always welcome. The male robin will fight to protect his patch of the garden or woodland.

On a sunny day in January you might see pairs of blue tits beginning to search for nest holes. When the trees are bare, you can see them in large groups. They often join up with other members of their family.

In America about 550 million redwing blackbirds will all roost together. If you counted one redwing per second, it would take you 17 years to count them all. How do you think anyone managed to count them?

A flock of starlings is an amazing sight. These speckled chatterboxes sleep on ledges on city buildings. Just before dusk they swarm together in tens of thousands before flying to their roosts. They stay together in summer too. The pairs nest in tree holes or on buildings.

Other birds flock together at any time of year. Look at the playing fields in winter, or large city squares. Which birds flock in these places?

Large flocks of birds are an amazing sight. But they can cause problems too. Farmers don't like them because they eat seeds and young plants in the fields. And in cities they can make a terrible mess on buildings and pavements.

Unusual birds

The small bird in this picture is a dunnock. It is feeding a young cuckoo that has taken over the nest

Cuckoos lay their eggs in other birds' nests. The cuckoo chooses the nests of small birds. She pushes out one egg so that hers will not be noticed. The cuckoo's egg usually hatches first. The fledgling pushes the other eggs out of the nest so that it can take all the food. The bird who built the nest cares for the young cuckoo as if it were her baby.

The crossbill is the only British bird which has the tips of its beak crossed. It walks sideways along the branches of conifer trees looking for fir cones. Crossbills eat the seeds which grow inside the cones and its beak is just right for picking them out.

The Arctic tern is the furthest traveller. It spends summer in the Arctic, flies to the Antarctic for summer there and then returns to the Arctic. The round trip is 40 thousand kilometres. That's so far that if you started walking and never stopped, it would take you over a year.

The bee humming bird is one of the smallest birds in the world. It is as small as a butterfly. Can you believe the bee humming bird's nest is the size of a thimble and her eggs are little bigger than a grain of rice?

mm   10   20   30   40   50   60

Night birds

While you are asleep some birds are awake. Owls rest during the day. At night they begin their hunt for food. Owls' large eyes can see better in poor light than our eyes can. They look for voles, mice and rats. They swoop down and snatch up these small creatures with their strong feet.

Tawny owl

Owl

'Who?
Who are you?
Who?'

    'I am owl,
    night's eyes,
    wise beyond understanding.'

'Who?
Who are you?
Who?'

    'I am owl,
    shadow of shadows,
    owner of forests,
    beautiful beyond comprehension.'

'Who?
Who are you?
Who?'

    'I am owl,
    plucker of moonbeams;
    owl, most mysterious.
    Beware.'

Patricia Hubbell

Glossary

clutch

The number of eggs that a bird lays and that the parent birds look after in the nest.

down feathers

Very soft, fluffy feathers.

extinct

When a type of creature, such as elephant birds or dinosaurs, no longer exists, we say it is 'extinct'. It means there are no more elephant birds or dinosaurs alive anywhere in the world.

flock

A flock is a large group of birds which stays together. You often see birds flying, feeding or perching in flocks.

sheen

The shine and gloss on a bird's feathers.

talons

A bird's sharp claws.